WEAPONS
OF THE
AMERICAN
REVOLUTION

BY JOHN HAMILTON

VISIT US AT
WWW.ABDOPUBLISHING.COM

Published by ABDO Publishing Company, PO Box 398166, Minneapolis, MN 55439. Copyright ©2013 by Abdo Consulting Group, Inc. International copyrights reserved in all countries. No part of this book may be reproduced in any form without written permission from the publisher. ABDO & Daughters™ is a trademark and logo of ABDO Publishing Company.

Printed in the United States of America, North Mankato, Minnesota.
122012
012013

♻ PRINTED ON RECYCLED PAPER

Editor: Sue Hamilton
Graphic Design: Sue Hamilton
Cover Design: Neil Klinepier
Cover: Painting by Don Troiani, www.historicalartprints.com
Interior Photos and Illustrations: AP-pgs 14-15, 20, 24 & 29; Corbis-pgs 11, 17, & 26-27; Getty-pgs 4-5; John Hamilton-pgs 8-9 & 25; Military and Historical Image Bank-pgs 3, 6-7, 10, 12, 13, 15 (pistol images), 16, 18 (sword), 19, 21, 22-23 & 31; Library of Congress-pg 1; U.S. Senate-pg 28; Wikimedia Commons-Photograph by Rama-pg 18 (spontoon).

ABDO Booklinks

To learn more about the American Revolution, visit ABDO Publishing Company online. Web sites about the American Revolution are featured on our Book Links pages. These links are routinely monitored and updated to provide the most current information available.
Web site: www.abdopublishing.com

Cataloging-in-Publication Data

Hamilton, John, 1959-
 Weapons of the American Revolution / John Hamilton.
  p. cm. -- (American Revolution)
Includes index.
ISBN 978-1-61783-683-1
1. United States--History--Revolution, 1775-1783--Weapons--Juvenile literature. I. Title.
973.7--dc22

2012945985

CONTENTS

WEAPONS OF THE AMERICAN REVOLUTION

Soldiers in the American Revolution fought a close and personal battle. Most were armed with flintlock muskets, although some carried pistols and rifles.

These early weapons did not shoot accurately from great distances. Usually, soldiers looked into the faces of their opponents before firing their weapons.

American soldiers of the Continental Army often battled Great Britain's Redcoats in hand-to-hand battles using bayonets, swords, axes, or spears. When a gun could only shoot once before needing to be reloaded, a handheld blade allowed a soldier to protect himself, and even continue fighting. Weapons of the American Revolution were simple, yet deadly.

Armed with muskets, rifles, pistols, and swords, the British Army and the Massachusetts militia meet during the Battle of Lexington on April 19, 1775.

MUSKETS

The main weapon used by soldiers of the American Revolution was the muzzle-loading flintlock musket. It was a smoothbore weapon, which meant the inside of the barrel—the part the bullet travels down—was smooth. When fired, loose-fitting ammunition bounced from side to side until it emerged from the barrel. The ammunition's bouncing motion greatly decreased the weapon's accuracy.

British soldiers were armed with a Land Pattern Musket, commonly called a "Brown Bess."

These .75-caliber flintlocks weighed about 10.5 pounds (4.8 kg), and were 58 inches (147 cm) long.

Since most colonists were required by British law to own firearms to fight when called, many Patriots also carried Brown Bess muskets.

American soldiers also used French-made Charleville .69-caliber muskets. They were often called French Pattern Muskets. Their smaller-caliber barrel meant less weight to be carried—only nine pounds (4.1 kg).

Muskets could have bayonets attached to the barrels for hand-to-hand combat. The stock was designed to be used as a club.

American militia armed with flintlock muskets in 1775.

A muzzle-loading musket fired only one shot at a time. Loading a musket was a cumbersome, multi-step process. Soldiers carried paper cartridges, with each cartridge holding a charge of powder and a round lead bullet.

A soldier could get off about three shots per minute. This could last for about four minutes before the musket's barrel became fouled and required cleaning.

Both the Brown Bess and the Charleville smoothbore muskets were only accurate to a distance of about 80-100 yards (73-91 m). Because muskets were so inaccurate, standard tactics called for officers to order their men to fire volleys of shots simultaneously toward the enemy. A deadly mass of lead balls was shot off by a row of soldiers standing shoulder to shoulder. After a row of soldiers fired, they moved off and a second row took their place, ready to fire a second volley. These volleys of bullets struck down many soldiers, causing gaps in the enemy line. Soldiers could then rush in using their bayonets, or other handheld weapons, for hand-to-hand combat. However, soldiers on the front lines were exposed to musket fire. Loss of life was great, even with inaccurate weapons.

When a soldier pulled the trigger of a flintlock musket, a hammer with a flint tip struck a metal plate, causing a spark. This spark ignited the gunpowder inside the barrel. The resulting explosion forced the lead ball-shaped bullet out of the barrel.

BAYONETS

In battle, line after line of musket-bearing soldiers stood shoulder to shoulder and fired at the enemy. The goal was to rain down musket balls and terror. Both the British Army and the American Continental Army used these same tactics.

The battlefield filled with bullets and blinding white smoke. The next step was to charge, or defend against the charge, with musket-mounted bayonets.

A bayonet was a long blade attached to the muzzle of a musket. It turned the firearm into a spear. Bayonets were used in close, hand-to-hand combat.

Triangle-shaped bayonets caused horrible tearing wounds. Victims often bled to death. Bayonets became a weapon of intimidation. Soldiers sometimes surrendered out of fear when pitted against an enemy charging with bayonets.

Bayonets were also used against cavalry troops. Soldiers on horseback were at an advantage when attacking enemy foot soldiers. Ground troops sometimes defended themselves by killing cavalry horses with bayonets. This forced cavalrymen to the ground to fight.

John Trumbull's painting The Death of General Warren at the Battle of Bunker Hill, June 17, 1775 *shows the horror of bayonet combat.*

RIFLES

If long-range accuracy was needed, riflemen were called in. Rifled barrels have spiral grooves cut on the inside. This causes the bullet to spin, greatly increasing accuracy. Instead of a smoothbore musket's range of 80-100 yards (73-91 m), a rifle could accurately hit a target 100-250 yards (91-229 m) away.

Snipers and scouts often carried rifles. Brigadier General Daniel Morgan of the Continental Army became famous for leading groups of rugged frontiersmen called "Morgan's Riflemen." They used accurate long rifles. Morgan was skilled at unconventional battlefield tactics. He ordered riflemen to shoot at British officers to create confusion. British officers were

A 1776 Pennsylvania Long Rifle.

soon advised to stop wearing their brightly colored gold uniform trimmings on the battlefield to avoid standing out as targets.

Although a rifle was quite accurate, it needed to be loaded carefully. Loose powder from a powder horn was inserted, along with a tight-fitting lead ball wrapped in a small piece of cloth. A rifleman could only fire one shot about every 90 seconds.

Another disadvantage was that rifles were not made to hold bayonets. A "plug bayonet," basically a knife with a wooden plug on one end, could be inserted into the barrel of a rifle. But this meant the rifle could no longer be fired. A rifleman often had to be protected by troops with muskets. Still, for precise shots, a rifle was the weapon of choice.

A Continental Army rifleman used the forest for cover while scouting or preparing for a sniping shot. Rifles were more accurate than muskets, but took longer to load.

PISTOLS

Pistols, small handheld firearms, were mostly carried by officers or mounted cavalrymen. They could be stored in a saddle holster, a pocket, or even a boot. Pistols were close-range weapons accurate to about 15 feet (4.6 m) or less. Like muskets and rifles, a pistol fired only one shot and then had to be reloaded. At best, a soldier could only fire two or three shots per minute. Pistols had little practical use in combat, except as last-minute protection at very close quarters.

Two types of pistols were commonly manufactured: heavy and light. A heavy dragoon pistol had a 12-inch (30.5-cm) barrel. The preferred light dragoon pistol was only 9 inches (23 cm) long. British, American, and French manufacturers created these personal weapons. They could be simple or very decorated and ornate. Overall, however, few soldiers counted on their pistols for anything but last-minute protection.

British Light Dragoon Pistol

American Holster Pistol

KNIVES, AXES, AND TOMAHAWKS

Many battles of the American Revolution came down to bloody, hand-to-hand combat. It took a long time to reload muskets and rifles. They weren't accurate weapons by today's standards, and they often misfired. By the time a soldier fired off a round and reloaded, the enemy could easily have charged forward for close-combat action. Soldiers always had to be ready to use backup weapons to defend themselves.

Most American soldiers were comfortable with knives, axes, and Native American-style tomahawks. These tools were often used to hunt and prepare game animals, or chop wood. They were also deadly weapons on the battlefield. Tomahawks could be used in several ways. One edge of the metal head cut like a knife, while the other side crushed like a hammer.

A simple knife could be used in a strong cutting or stabbing attack, while the long handles of axes and tomahawks added leverage and power to the stroke. Additionally, axes and tomahawks could be thrown short distances.

A U.S.-emblazoned tomahawk.

In close hand-to-hand combat, bladed
weapons such as knives, axes,
and tomahawks allowed soldiers
with single-shot firearms to defend
themselves. Native American allies
for both the Continental Army and the
British Army were skilled in the use of
tomahawks.

SABERS, SWORDS, AND SPEARS

Lion-Headed Sword

Sabers and swords were carried by ranking officers, sergeants, and cavalrymen. A cavalryman might carry a pistol or short rifle called a musketoon, but the mounted soldier often considered his saber or broadsword to be his main weapon.

General George Washington, commander of the American Continental Army, felt that an officer equipped with a firearm might be distracted from his true duties of commanding his troops. Washington ordered

Spontoon

that officers carry spontoons. These 6.5-foot (2-m) -long spears were topped with sharp, sometimes decorative, metal heads. Officers could also use spontoons as signaling devices for their troops.

Halberds were similar to spontoons. They were long, two-handed poles used by ranking members of the British Army. The halberd consisted of a spear point melded atop a battle-ax head. The curved back blade was originally created to pull a soldier off a horse.

18

An American mounted cavalryman from the 3rd Continental Light Dragoons.

ARTILLERY

Artillery weapons included heavy guns (cannons), howitzers, and mortars. They were often used to defend and defeat forts during the American Revolution. Warships were armed with cannons designed to batter and destroy. Field cannons could kill dozens of enemy troops at once.

The British Army was much better supplied with these types of heavy weapons. In 1775, at the start of the war, the American objective during several battles was to capture British cannons, ammunition, and gunpowder.

The Patriots received a huge boost in May 1775 with the capture of British-held Fort Ticonderoga by the combined forces of Generals Benedict Arnold and Ethan Allen. The northeastern New York state stronghold was a storehouse of heavy artillery and ammunition.

The captured weapons were sorely needed to defend Boston, Massachusetts. Henry Knox, a Boston bookstore owner, devised a plan to move the artillery, which General Washington quickly approved.

Knox was given the rank of colonel and became part of the newly formed Continental Regiment of Artillery. He arrived at Fort Ticonderoga on December 5, 1775.

After floating the captured artillery across Lake George by flat-bottomed boat, Knox's men built sledges, sturdy sleds with runners. In late December, about 50 artillery pieces were loaded onto the sledges, and teams of oxen began towing the 60 tons (54 metric tons) of weapons over the frozen New England landscape. Knox's "noble train of artillery" arrived in Boston several weeks later.

A private in Knox's Continental Regiment of Artillery stands guard in front of a cannon.

A cannon's maximum range was about 2,000 yards (1,829 m). Its effective range was about 1,000 yards (914 m).

Americans captured British artillery when they could. They also bought French cannons, and increased production of their own weapons. They made cannons from both iron, which was cheap but very heavy, and bronze, which resulted in lighter but more expensive weapons.

Cannons were made in 13 different calibers, or sizes, during the American Revolution. Their names were based on the weight of the solid iron ball that was shot, not on how much the cannon itself weighed. For example, a 3-pounder cannon fired a 3-pound (1.4-kg) ball. The most common cannons used during the war were 3-, 6-, 8-, and 12-pounders.

Heavier-weight cannons were used to destroy forts. Lighter-weight cannons were used mainly against soldiers on the battlefield. A 3-pounder cannon could be mounted on wheels and easily transported to battle by a single horse. If necessary, several men could move a 3-pounder overland.

Cannons fired several types of ammunition. Solid shot iron balls were used to destroy wooden structures or even enemy artillery. Cannons also fired hollow bombs. Black powder was poured into the shell and a fuse was lit. Several seconds after landing, the bomb exploded. Canister and grape shot were round balls of lead or iron packed in either a metal can or a cloth bag.

A British Army Royal Artillery Gunner stands guard next to a cannon.

Grape shot projectiles were golfball-sized. They were usually used by navy ships. Canister shot were marble-sized, and used by the army. At close range, these weapons sprayed multiple projectiles onto the battlefield, killing or wounding many enemy soldiers at once.

A mortar's maximum range was about 1,400 yards (1,280 m). Its effective range was about 750 yards (686 m).

A Revolutionary War mortar at Yorktown Battlefield in Virginia.

Mortars are small cannons with short barrels, usually mounted on sturdy wooden platforms or sleds. They were designed to lob bombs high into the air, often over the top of a fort's walls or down onto the deck of a ship. Mortars were used by both armies and navies during the American Revolution.

Mortars differed from cannons in that they had a powder chamber in the back. The elevation of the gun remained mostly the same. What varied was the amount of powder charge that went into the chamber. The greater the charge, the farther the range of the shell.

Howitzers were similar to mortars except they were more mobile. Howitzers fired bombs high into the air. A gunpowder-filled ball, lit by a fuse, soared above troops on the ground. If the timing was right, the bomb's explosion took place right above the soldiers, raining fiery debris down on the enemy.

A howitzer's maximum range was about 1,300 yards (1,189 m). Its effective range was about 750 yards (686 m).

WARSHIPS

In 1775, at the start of the American Revolution, Great Britain had the most powerful navy on Earth. The Royal Navy ruled the seas with its mighty ships of the line. These were multi-deck vessels bristling with between 74 and 120 guns (cannons). They were called ships of the line because in battle they formed a single line to batter the enemy with continuous broadside attacks.

The Royal Navy also used smaller ships called frigates. They only carried between 20 and 36 guns on one or two decks, but frigates were much faster and more maneuverable than ships of the line.

Despite their impressive ships and sailors, the Royal Navy had difficulty patrolling America's long coastline. British ships were most effective in blocking supplies from entering some ports, and in supporting ground troop operations.

British warships were victorious during the Battle of Cape St. Vincent on January 16, 1780, during the American Revolution.

The Continental Navy began in Philadelphia, Pennsylvania, with the Continental Congress's decision to purchase armed vessels on October 13, 1775. Ships, captains, sailors, and weapons all had to be found, outfitted, and trained. Rhode Island's Esek Hopkins was named naval commander-in-chief.

The first commissioned ship, the USS *Alfred*, was armed with 20 9-pounder and 10 6-pounder smoothbore cannons. Next came the USS *Columbus*, a 28-gun ship. By the end of 1776, the Continental Navy consisted of 27 ships that included frigates, brigantines, sloops, and schooners. An additional 31 vessels were obtained during the course of the American Revolution. Four were borrowed from France. Outmatched by the Royal Navy's ships, the Continental Navy's goals were to capture enemy warships and supplies, and to harass King George's commercial vessels.

John Paul Jones

On September 23, 1779, Captain John Paul Jones of the 42-gun frigate USS *Bonhomme Richard* fought the British man-of-war HMS *Serapis* off the coast of England. At first, the more powerful *Serapis* battered the *Bonhomme Richard*. The British captain called out for Jones to surrender. Jones replied, "Sir, I have not yet begun to fight!"

True to his word, Jones was victorious and eventually captured the *Serapis*. Sadly, the badly damaged *Bonhomme Richard* sank two days later. However, the battle reflected the strength, determination, and cunning of the American Patriots. They were ready to fight against all odds to win their freedom and form a new nation.

The USS *Bonhomme Richard* fights the British man-of-war HMS *Serapis*. When the British captain called for Captain John Paul Jones to surrender, he is famously quoted as saying, "Sir, I have not yet begun to fight!"

GLOSSARY

ARTILLERY
Large weapons of war, such as cannons, mortars, and howitzers, that are used by military forces on land and at sea.

CAVALRY
During the American Revolution era, soldiers who rode and fought on horseback were called cavalry. Modern cavalry includes soldiers who fight in armored vehicles such as tanks or attack helicopters.

DRAGOON
Mounted infantry troops who rode on horseback, but often fought on foot.

FLINTLOCK
A weapon such as a musket, rifle, or pistol, which is fired using the flintlock system created in the early 1600s. When the firearm's trigger is pulled, a hammer with a flint tip strikes a metal plate, causing a spark. This spark ignites the gunpowder inside the barrel. The resulting explosion forces the lead ball-shaped bullet out of the barrel.

MILITIA
Citizens who were part-time soldiers rather than professional army fighters. Militiamen, such as the Minutemen from Massachusetts, usually fought only in their local areas and continued with their normal jobs when they were not needed.

MISFIRE
When a loaded firearm fails to shoot a bullet after the trigger is pulled.

MUSKET

A single-shot weapon, fired from the shoulder, that resembles a modern rifle. Muskets have smooth bores (the inside of the barrel). Their accuracy and range were limited, but a volley of muskets from a large group of soldiers could be quite deadly.

PATRIOTS

Colonists who rebelled against Great Britain during the American Revolution.

POWDER HORN

A container that holds and dispenses gunpowder. Original powder horns were made from the horns of animals such as cows or oxen. The wide end is blocked off. The narrow end, out of which the gunpowder is poured, has a removable plug.

REDCOATS

The name that was often given to British soldiers because part of their uniform included a bright red coat.

RIFLED BARREL

Rifled barrels have spiral grooves cut on the inside of the barrel—the part that the bullet travels down. The grooves cause the bullet to spin. Rifling greatly increases the accuracy of a weapon.

SMOOTHBORE BARREL

Smoothbore weapons are constructed with barrels—the part the bullet travels down—that are smooth. When the weapon is fired, the loose-fitting ammunition bounces from side to side until it emerges from the barrel. The bullet's motion greatly decreases the weapon's accuracy.

INDEX